7/07

D1240650

THE ARCHITECTURE OF LANGUAGE

The Architecture
of Language

POEMS

QUINCY TROUPE

COFFEE HOUSE PRESS
MINNEAPOLIS
2006

COPYRIGHT © 2006 Quincy Troupe
COVER & BOOK DESIGN Linda S. Koutsky
COVER PAINTING © Al Loving
COVER ART PHOTOGRAPH Shawn Walker
AUTHOR PHOTOGRAPH © Michael Jones

Coffee House Press books are available to the trade through our primary distributor, Consortium Book Sales & Distribution, 1045 Westgate Drive, Saint Paul, MN 55114. For personal orders, catalogs, or other information, write to: Coffee House Press, 27 North Fourth Street, Suite 400, Minneapolis, MN 55401.

Coffee House Press is a nonprofit literary publishing house. Support from private foundations, corporate giving programs, government programs, and generous individuals helps make the publication of our books possible. We gratefully acknowledge their support in detail in the back of this book.

Good books are brewing at coffeehousepress.org

LIBRARY OF CONGRESS CATALOGING-IN-PUBLICATION DATA
Troupe, Quincy.
The architecture of language : poems / by Quincy Troupe.
p. cm.
ISBN-13: 978-1-56689-189-9 (alk. paper)
ISBN-10: 1-56689-189-2 (alk. paper)
ISBN-13: 978-1-56689-190-5 (pbk. : alk. paper)
ISBN-10: 1-56689-190-6 (pbk. : alk. paper)
I. Title.
PS3570.R63A73 2006
811'.54—DC22
2006012061

FIRST EDITION | FIRST PRINTING
1 3 5 7 9 8 6 4 2
Printed in Canada

ACKNOWLEDGMENTS
Some of these poems first appeared in the following journals and magazines: *New Letters, The American Poetry Review, The Green Magazine,* and *Drumvoices.*

DEDICATION

This book is dedicated to my mother, Dorothy Smith Marshall;
the memory of my father, Quincy Trouppe Sr.;
the memories of my grandmothers, Leona Smith and Mary Troupe;
and my wife, Margaret Porter Troupe.

I would also like to acknowledge Micheline and Luc Michaux-Vignes;
Maryse Conde; Richard Philcox; Christian Amour;
the Basses family: Heric, Daniel and his wife Jacquline;
Nicole and Jacques-Marie; Dr. Christian St. Martin and his wife Lidie;
John "Monk" Nanga, his sister Ghislane and her soul mate Luther Francois;
Klod Kravué; and Luigy Lucides for providing safe and loving
harbors in Guadeloupe.

.

CONTENTS

1.

2.

3.

4.

5.

6.

7.

.

THE ARCHITECTURE OF LANGUAGE

1.

EGGPLANTS: A FABLE

for Brinden

her mother told her she was growing egg-
plants, she was eight years old,
with an active imagination, blooming amongst trolls
& other homegrown demons, who played under
the bridge down the street,

the trolls lived in little houses
on the hill, over the pacific, in la jolla,
down the street from the demons who all lived
inside little brinden's active imagination,

her mother, a botanist, grew the vegetables
the family ate, while her father was a storyteller who told
the scary tall tales
that scared little brinden's eyes to bug out
at the dinner table
with each meal,

at breakfast,
little brinden dreamed of plucking eggs
from her mother's vine, dreamed
of helping her make tostados, omelettes, huevos rancheros,
eggs benedict, boiling little white eggs into prim perfection,
where they would sit, plump, waiting on her plate,
before she sank her perfect white teeth into them,
after cracking their fragile shells
into fault lines that looked like veins running
like rivers up her grandmother's arms & legs,

so each & every morning she would watch
beneath her window her mother's vine,
where she said her egg-

                              plants would bloom

& as the hard little buds grew & grew
past the size of little eggs little brinden knew
her wonderment grew
& she became more worried with each passing day,
then when the hard green buds

                                        started turning purple,
wearing the odd long nose of an anteater
little brinden saw in a picture book
she became very scared & worried,

then one day the oversized ugly something
dropped off the vine & lay like a plump dead rat
beneath her window,

                                          only it had no eyes,
was definitely not the primp, plump egg
she had long so dreamed of biting into,

now brinden was baffled into silence,
intrigued by the mystery before her
there, plopped on the ground she broke the silence,
remembered to ask her mother the question
she had carried in her head since she first saw
her egg going bad, turning into something other
than her mind's eye told her was true,

was it a troll or demon, like the ones living
under the bridge down the winding narrow street,

but that fantasy couldn't be true,
                                        didn't hold water,
because they lived down there, under the bridge,
& her imagination had no place in it for this
ratlike thing down there, under *her* window—

that place was reserved for her *egg*,

so she asked, "mother, what was it you said
you were growing on the vine underneath my window?"

"eggplants," her mother said, "eggplants,
   what did you think I said?"

"never mind," little brinden said, "never mind,"

but in her eight-year-old dreams she still saw eggs
growing on her mother's vine underneath her window,
still saw trolls & demons disappearing under the bridge
when the sun sank down into the pacific,
fronting the hillsides of la jolla

VICHYSSOISE

you always liked the word, *vichyssoise*,
the way it sounded, rolled around
your tongue, was a puzzle, an adventure,
the way it sent your mind flying off in space,
wondering where all those different chic
sounds came from, fishy sea syllables swishing
inside your mouth like wishes, then yeasting off
endings, as in a jimi hendrix wah-wah riff,
the word brought to mind soirees,
colors swirling around in space,

then you found out it was a soup of leeks
& potatoes, creamy cold stuff—
you didn't like anything creamy in those days—
ending your romance with eating the word,
though you still loved the sound, the hissing articulation
of pissing three syllables, tacked on to a vixen's breath
at the beginning of the word,
a woman ordering cheese in the middle,
closing with an ah sound with a little fizz,

today, you write a poem about the way
the word swishes through the air evoking
a shopping list of haute cuisine attitudes,
connects with your ear, it's all so very pleasant now,
though you still haven't been able to stomach the cold,
highfalutin creamy soup so many care for, yet
you give thanks to whoever whipped the chilly stuff up,

gave it its handle, so it could finesse its way,
skimming through lips with its clever, twisting pitches,
sound whispering light as three sea waves crawling in,
quiet as foam soaking into hot sand under the sun's
tongue, is a hissing, sleight-of-hand, tricky-sliding
word, an anapest in its accentual-syllabic prosody,
so right, so hoity-toity, so upper class,

you can drop it at high-end parties with people
who care about such things, you can think

you're in the hip crowd, though some may wonder
why you never raise even one spoonful of the white,
cold stuff to your lips, even though you pronounce
the word like a native, like an initiate—

can you say vish-she-swaaz?

HAIKU SCENES

faces of leaves fall
red as kisses stamped on cheeks,
pile up brown on streets,

as pine needles wave
outside my window, dance slow
scherzos on the wind,

the landscape green here,
dazzling, bird-calling colors,
fragrant la jolla,

lavender ice plants
explode on hillsides in spring,
glistening with green,

my thoughts reach out blue,
look like the ocean when viewed
high up in the sky,

also blue when viewed
from down here, whispering trees
remind of sea waves

lapping rocks, spent brown
leaves crumbling in winter's cold,
skeins of words flying,

geese in summer skies,
kites, their strings unraveling,
planes up in the blue

2.

VERSACE

eye watch my cat, versace, roll over on her back,
four paws boxing the air, she is striking there,
soft white, brown striped & spotted fur,
with the coat of a small leopard, she is beautiful flipping
& flopping, her tail up & down, stretching
her long, lean body outside my window, in the sun,
blue eyes opening & closing as she naps

                                                in a world of her own, at first glance
she seems so innocent when she yawns, revealing
those long white nail-like fangs hinting at the possible
terror she is when she awakens,

suddenly she is alert, her ears twitching & turning around
like crazed antennas, then tensing she leaps quick as a cobra striking,
uncoiling in midair, strikes some hapless victim
she was clocking while she appeared to be dozing
& it's all over in a blink except for the futile, spasmodic twitching,
the horrible death struggle, then she eats the thing whole,
licks her paw, scratches behind her ear, then
stretches out again & goes back to dozing,

but don't get me wrong, she's a beautiful, loving friend
inside the house, always giving of her love freely,
but outside, in the air—even inside if it's a shadow that moves—
watch out, especially if you're a tasty bird, rat, or lizard,

watch out, you'll pay the ultimate price for not paying attention,
sleeping on the job, it will be all over quicker than the blink
of an eye glazing over, or closing, in death

A CONVENTION OF LITTLE DOGS

in manhattan's central park, on a cold, bright day
in november, a convention of little dogs swirl,
dart around sparse grass in a clearing, pick their way
through tangled heaps of fallen bone-branches
felled by fierce onslaughts of howling alaskan winds
that sliced through clothing like razors the night before,
today, eye'm out for my morning stroll, see these tiny,
pampered creatures—chihuahuas, poodles, lapdogs—
fit snugly in their little fur coats, ribbons on their heads,
in their ears, who prance around prissy on itty-bitty feet
like haughty ballet dancers up on their toes, aflutter,
with big attitudes, nose-in-the-air, picky, prickly royalty who start
after all their busy fussing to get on their masters' nerves,
they command them to sit—after all, they're the ones paying
for all these silly little perks—allow them to finish their own fussy
business, this gets on the little royals' nerves—especially
the ground's cold touch on their delicate tiny bottoms—
so the little snits start bitching in their high-pitched, rapid-fire,
machine-gun pissing, brittle, shrill wolf-ticket-selling
voices, snipping & sniping at everything passing by,
even other masters, not to mention huge menacing dogs—
dobermans, german shepherds, pit bulls—who strut
their own bold confident stuff, their power to kill, but today
they're minding their own sullen business until the petite royals
remind them what's at stake—after all, it's a power game
being played out everywhere today—& these big muckademutts,
kingpins on the block, don't like being snipped at by impudent
small things—fleas & gnats to them—buzzing around on

mosquito-sized clickedy-click feet, bejeweled, manicured nails,
as if they ruled the world instead of these big dogs,
who don't like listening to all this busy bric-a-brac,
little nattering from these nervy, posturing irritants,
with the gall to think they can challenge the muckademutts'
supreme authority with their simpering, prissy, uppity fussing—
all this gets on a big dog's nerves—so they expose fierce teeth,
draw back lips into snarls, fix their fangs into snit-traps,
awesome snares, scare barks back down throats
of these little busybodies, who are nothing but royal little knick-
knacks for big dogs, morning snacks for these humongous jaws,
wide open now, they turn these pretentious royal pretenders back
to the cowards they really are, whimpering at a real show
of force—isn't this what happens most places in the world
today?—& eye, just a witness to it all, a poetic chronicler,
eye keep walking through the day, snapping images,
picking up sounds eye develop into figurative language,
always alert, grateful for new york's free ideas & drama

3.

FEAR

eye sit up nights sweating, waiting
for a coral snake to slither through
my bed with its tiny mouth
                   full of deadly fangs,
though eye have no proof it's there
somehow it lives inside my head
down here at the atlantic arts center,
eye carry my flashlight around at night
when eye go out,
                  watch its white bone light
probing through dense bushes,
where fear tells my mind the snake is,
there, arched like a rainbow finger
of a witch, or sorcerer, beckoning me,
seducing me,
                 a deadly siren calling
sweet from that deep dark space
surrounded by mystery, myth,
the alluring power of the unknown

FOURTEEN DOORS AT COMSTOCK PRISON
A DIRGE-CHANT

for Joseph Bruchac, Hamiet Bluiett, & Margaret

1.

fourteen doors clanged shut at comstock prison
fourteen doors between fresh blue sky & me
fourteen doors shell-shocked my spirit at comstock
fourteen doors between freedom & me
your kisses sweet with me, at comstock

it was late afternoon when we came to the ominous silence
late afternoon stricken with a wheezing sun dying in the west
late afternoon when the tall lengthening shadow loomed terrible
before us, late afternoon filled with frozen february weather

& fourteen doors sounded a death toll on silence
fourteen doors & voices shocked fearing into drowning
fourteen doors & a killer guard steely beside us

fourteen doors between your soft brown eyes & me

2.

long corridors of whispers greet us, distance slammed shut
swallowed us as ringing echoes reverberated
throughout my flesh & hunger thundered chords of blues tones
as fever stitched into our eyes behind these walls, spilled over us
taking our breath away in this suffocating space

cold eyes bright as sun reflecting off razor blades turned sullen
as smoldering coals, tested my very best under duress
& plunder, no love lost found as rage wheeled & turned on its heels
with no feeling for love of what courage can be
but everything spent here for what is needed in the moment
nothing more, nothing less, fear all around us

& fourteen doors locked me back into black memory
fourteen doors unlocked years of tears stunned by silent absence
fourteen doors & my dreams thirsty for long-gone faces
fourteen doors between your flesh & my spirit, margaret

fourteen doors evoke so many empty spaces & places
fourteen doors evoke so many spaces where faces once rested

HISTORICAL MOMENT

after a lynching whites
would cut down the branch
where the "strange fruit" hung,
paint the trunk of the tree
red as blood flowing
from the tortured severed head,
its grimacing lips forever mute,
open, in a perfect O,
until flesh falls away, leaves
only leering teeth & bone

THE HOURS FLY QUICK

the hours fly quick on wings of clipped winds
like nonsense blown from mouths of hot air—
people—including my own—form syllables, suds,
words shot through pursed lips like greased sleaze
& bloom inside all these rooms dominated by television's
babble sluicing idiot images invented in modern test tubes—
clones—blinking, slathering all over controlled airwaves
of an up-for-sale world, blinking a paucity of spirit,
so dance you leering ventriloquists, marionettes,
you greedy counterfeits, dance, dance, dance

POLITICIANS & SHOW BUSINESS

seems like before you can say "boo" they're back
selling their three-ring circus, ringmasters, fronting slick
con men, women, too, clowns & decoys, midgets & giants,
flame-eating anorexics from transylvania, jugglers
tossing red, white, & blue balls into the lights,
gyrating acrobats, high-wire-walking
flimflams dishing jive & gab like short-order cooks
taking orders from whoever pays the bill,

                                           they are gyrating

houdinis, reveal a gift for gab, are used-car dealers, they
sometimes remind me of shyster boxing promoters, hawkers
at the county fair selling cakes, with chances to throw the ring
over bottlenecks, mack-men, big-time preachers
under big tents, purveyors of dreams,

                                       every two, or four years

it's time for these manipulators to show high-octane love
to special interest groups, pay attention to bug-eyed babies,
hold them up cooing & kicking for crowds to see
while they mimic baby coos for shadow-catching cameras,
"coochie-coochie-coo"

                         the jugglers drool, then, quick as a blink
before infants flip their switches,

start bawling & screaming at the top of their lungs,
in front of an audience of voters, our ringmasters-jugglers-

escape artists are like star quarterbacks
handing off babies to parents in the nick of time,

because no seasoned politician wants to be caught dead
holding some red-faced screaming baby on the six o'clock news,
no-sir-re bob, it's bad for their public image,

it's like miles davis once said,
                              "it's all about style & timing,"

in the whirr of shuttlebugs & make believe,
when you're followed around like a sports star,
or famous actor, which a few of them are, some good, some bad,
as they run around with lips flapping the political gospel, divide
& conquer, say whatever polls tell them to,
stay on message, at all cost, please
don't tell the truth if it hurts the base,

they better have great timing, be stylish too, be able

to prattle on about whatever people *want* to hear,
they set fires for smoke screens, disguise all their movements,
jump through hoops, become chameleons,
                              flash clean, white pearlies,

make sure their hairdos are combed, toupees in place—
& for god's sake don't wear a crooked wig in front of a camera—
wear clean pressed suits, a shirt & tie—it's great if it's red
white & blue—& for women demure, conservative
dresses will do, pants too if they're not too body-clinging,
something nondescript,

nothing too revealing, don't ever show cleavage
& always wear a small american flag

somewhere everybody can see

& always remember to mention God,
                    Jesus Christ, & God bless America,

because dealing with the public's fickle sense of morality
& taste ain't no joke
            & you never know what will set off their alarm bells,

so just keep on looking important to flummoxed constituents

& you can bet on hauling away duffle bags full of cash
as long as you keep on bewitching the people

with fluctuating, contradictory—"don't hold me to it"—
messages with a slippery gift of gab—they always play well

like an old scratched-up popular phonograph record

the ones the flummoxed masses of people always
want to hear, you know—the oldies but goodies—

the ones show-biz politicians remember & know so well

THE TIMES WE LIVE IN

suddenly balls of fire, billowing black smoke turning
into snake-tails the color of ash, rises up to heaven,
corkscrewing, whispering, as in prayer,
suddenly screams, moans, body parts flying, bloody hands
here, severed feet & toes there, torsos with no heads, brains
splattered as collages on walls, dead eyes of children stare,
blown out of heads, an ear here, a nose there, two lips
on a wall perfectly shaped, pursed, as if about to kiss,
gunfire stitching periods throughout sentences
written across quaking, stenciled chests, bodies twitching
on television screens, up close, bombs leaving wreckage,
eyeballs & cameras snap wholesale carnage, print
imitations of paintings on the sides of buses,
postcards from haiti, in the middle east brutal scenes show
graphically the moments we live in, instances of madness,
pure, cold depravity witnessed as acts in countless horror
films, video games freezing the focus of our children
at home in the cyberspace world, internet cafés
packed all over the world, massacres sold, unfolding genocides
played out in war games on computer screens,
dictate, perhaps, how young people know their hearts,
whether they feel a chill when pulling triggers in games,
in the real world, see graphic blood splattering
everywhere inside worlds of small screens, watch body parts
flying off like pieces of shrapnel, our love for each other,
the human condition, shattered as pieces of steel
exploded from hand grenades, are souvenirs
thrown into gatherings, delivered in this brutal age,
are postcards sent, kisses thrown from tortured hearts

THREE SEVENS: 21 LINES HOPING FOR CHANGE

an opaque sky streaks tears down from clouds
on the other side of murmuring
a language understood by flies
after decomposition has been broken becomes
clear syllables rolling again from a bird's vibrating tongue
& music is heard by those who recognize its beauty
when sound penetrates love to beating hearts

listen to the antiphonal flow coursing up
from rivers of ancestors a breathing history lives there
to know the secret mysteries voiced within codes
you must first feel the poet's lashing words
you have buried deep inside sleep their resonance
under pitch-black clouds of acrid amnesia
you have forgotten even the sound of your name

ghoulish apparitions of flames dance under shadows now
spreading umbrellas of smoke billowing wings over hunger
advance through the world like pestilential plagues
nuclear as evil intentions of men with unchecked power
unleashed under guises of unholy gospels
& lethal when pulpits are aligned with bullets
& guns put in the hands of praying congregations

SHARED POEM

organizing against the war
in iraq in america
is like trying to stir heavy
concrete with an eyelash

THE SIGNATURES OF TIME

binding signatures of time are fading footprints
tracking across wind-blown desert floors,

newspapers whipping down cold, empty streets,
split apart, become wings sailing like stingrays
swimming through wash of an emerald sea,

history is moments gleaned from unsorted stacks
holding facts, voices steamed clean as mussels
on a plate, disintegrating on worn tapes,
splintering on spools in old tape recorders,

like photos fading out in yellowing newspapers

EYE AM FOREVER
LOOKING FOR SHADOWS

eye am always looking for shadows dropping hints
where they lost their old bodies, is a matter open
to question, a conjecture full of mystery,

eye am watching for bird wings eye imagine
are eyebrows over two moons in a blind man's face,

now my ti punch is speaking to me
full of rum, limes, sugar, & gingembre, in a language
full of zouk, clear blue-green caribbean water,

it reminds me of the translucence of my cat's eyes,

now the moments are filled with hesitations,
the sounds exploding in music so quickly
they remind me of skiers blowing down mountain slopes
slick with hard ice & snow,

but who are we fooling during these frivolous moments
slick with silly infomercials flooding
the language we speak, created in test tubes,

what is the drilling sound we hear inside our heads,
the loud jackhammer of woodpeckers tapping out
thoughts with hard sharp beaks like machine-gun fire
ricocheting off walls & exploding skulls,

it's time now to pay attention to where this creaking
boat is taking us, leaking, taking on water as it goes,
it's time to get nervous about not being nervous,

because if you're not jumpy you aren't paying attention
about being worried, aren't giving consideration
to being edgy as a crash & burn man absent cocaine,

you're not paying attention while entire worlds burn

A POEM FOR ALL SO-CALLED HALF-BREEDS:
THE LEGACY, A SLOW TURNING

for my grandmothers, Leona Smith and Mary Troupe

1.

a cross-fertilization of blood
these days of nailing rain
these days of skint-back midnights & nightmares
we come sin-tight, with our bubas & war feathers
to edges of deafening silence
to watch the electrocution of night sin-tight
to watch spent midnights swallow stars
& listen to the plunging deep silence
reminding me of an eighteen-minute tape gap
rewinding through the thickening absences
& shadows stitching through
recesses of our brains

                    & so we cancel mind flights through space
take our flesh down to worn undertakers
blow out the lights of the night

& if eye came to know
the meaning of dusk-fall's karintha flesh & rhythm
came to know the grammar beneath
these blood-stained ancestors' names
eye think eye would know the sound
space / music makes between echoes
would come to know these unfinished sounds
ping-ponging back between

these words as echoes
between these cadences of flames

eye would hear & know the stark
grim beauty of air-cupping skulls resting on sand
the tongue-folding lyricism of my fused so-called
half-breed grandmothers' hands
sweet faces turning their eyes inward
beyond even the blues heard at sunsets

& if eye came to know the beauty
the bone-deep legacy of cherokee & african
the cross-fertilization of bubas & war feathers
the cross-fertilization of whip & buffalo
the veined twin legacy coursing through the blood
nourishing the roots of my double-veined name
it would not be enough to erase the pain
of the butchered, faceless shadows
dancing through recesses of my brain

2.

these days fro-
zen red suns are nails hammered into tongues
into palms creased with latticework of rivers
crosses hung around necks
burnt into brains dug into the red earth
holding black christ figures eyes gouged out hands chopped off
missing genitalia & the rage deep as bone marrow
twisting slowly as knives sunk into bellies
as dark silhouettes in black pine trees

rooted in the bloodthirsty soil of georgia & tennessee
twist slowly there, ever so slowly, like dirges or funeral chants
the dark silhouettes turning in trees
black pine trees in georgia & tennessee
under a black sky breaking silence in missouri
with hand thunderclaps cracking over drenching red
hound dogs soaked leaves
the bloodthirsty soil of georgia & tennessee

& this slow twisting & turning beyond
even what the blues of guitars can tell us
can cancel out beyond the glass-crowned walls of language
beyond metaphors coursing through this searching poem
only silence has heard the complete horror
only silence can tell us of the true pain

(& just today, grandmothers, O beautiful spirits
eye tried eating the pain away with chinese fried food
tried talking to a near-white-black-skinned-red-fool
who had been going to his own funeral
every day after he had his brain taken away—
he lives in his dreams in england
sips tea at four o'clock each afternoon
wearing cotton white gloves—
clean as a lobotomizing surgeon's scalpel
just before an operation—
wears two clear monocles over both eyes
waxes his mustache into two curving saber points
his breath a funky delirious wind of cat shit dogma
but murderous as king cobra whims)

& O the color of this pain is bougainvillea

the bloodthirsty soil of georgia & tennessee
the juju shaman man slurring blues at a ruby moon
the bloodthirsty soil of georgia & tennessee

look at the whip scars & cat-o'-nine-tail slashes
cut deep into prairies of memory's face
remember the dark silhouettes turning slowly in trees
in mountains of georgia & tennessee
thunderclaps of grief cracking the close air there
remember the blood-covered hound dogs   soaked leaves
the bloodthirsty soil of georgia & tennessee
the drooping silhouettes twisting
& turning slowly there as memory
as memory   as memory

the bloodthirsty soil of georgia & tennessee

3.

& so these days eye say juba
these incensed days of bougainvillea
eye say now beautiful red flowers like my blood
eye say eye juju the pain of my faceless shadow
eye say eye juju the blues like a baby lawrence tap dancer
eye say eye bring duane niatum juju to this poem
eye say eye bring joy harjo magic of buffalo skulls
to this poem eye bring moon faces hovering over the prairie
wearing war bonnets eye bring hoodoo to this poem
a sacred dance drummed down through pain
the scrubbed bone legacy of a name baptized in fire
to cleanse this genocidal nightmare of demonic white dreams

eye bring erzulie with her saltwater to wash clean
these white schemes these disintegrating dreams

4.

& so these days grandmothers wear robes of sunlight
despite the sound of perfectly drilled clean eye pits
despite the sound of air-cupping skullcaps resting on sand
holding history under stabbing moon knives
the legacy wrapped in silence of a cocked gun & shining bones
leering under river water there is a memory is a song
despite the hammered red sons & hammered black sons this is
a song of cross-fertilized sons as dialectical sons is a poem filled
with hammered nailed tongues we know now is a language long
buried underground as moon yellow screams of bones
moon yellow sounds of our ancestral bones grandmothers

their images silhouetted there among glinting knives
& rippling shadows among ping-ponging black pine trees
their leaves filigreeing over the dead raped woman's face
her skirt thrown back as a blanket over her body
(as they raped the soil of america & africa
as they still rape the womb of the earth)
eye hear now the moon-yellow sound of those echoes clearly
now the blood on the moon-yellow bones of our ancestors
is that raped body buried deep inside language of cross-fertilized
grammar is a song grandmothers is this poem

& O the color of this poem is bougainvillea
the bloodthirsty soil of georgia & tennessee
the juju slurring blues shaman man

singing with his guitar at a ruby moon
the bloodthirsty soil of georgia & tennessee

5.

& so these days eye remember
the bone-deep legacy felt
in the twin coursing rivers of my veins
these days a slow turning toward simple recognition
these days a slow turning toward fire toward secrets
coded in language these days
a slow turning inward
toward you tree-rooted grandmothers eye celebrate
your eyes gone beyond even sunsets
beyond fire-carrying beauty eye celebrate your secrets
coded where the lyricism of this blues meets
the legacy of sky thunder

the legacy held there
in your folded wrinkled hands grandmothers
the legacy held there for me to remember
is both you grand women grand-
mothers to celebrate & remember you
forever the duality of your dialectical
indian-african blood
grandmothers
the legacy held there
is you is you
the legacy held there

is finally me

4.

MEMORY AS A CIRCLE: FOR THE LOVE EYE LOST IN HURRICANE AUDREY

because it is beyond midnight somewhere,
between total darkness & daybreak,
light, pure & simple is
an echo of someone hidden far back in memory,
an echo pulsating like a heartbeat here with intensity,
like a drummer keeping time alive,
it follows the rhythms of an artist breathing
music through a face jumping from a canvas, extends itself
into a future you can't even see now but know
is there, perhaps, a moon sliding slowly across
the geography of black skin that is sky, is like a notion
a pearl once evoked in the mind when it first saw it coming,
it was a globe lit up like the round gleaming eye of a panther,
the idea of a black hole imploding with light
was your smile, love, come here again back from memory
seducing, a light pulsating through imitates your face,
where you once were, all these years
where a hole shaped like a cutout of you
flattened itself out daily inside my longing

& eye see a fire burning way out there in the pitch-
black desert of midnight,
perhaps it is a campfire encircled by lonely spirits back when
eye knew you as a deep-sea diving lover, always underwater,
entombed inside your own breath, your silent voice
now a chain-link of bubbles climbing forever upward

toward the surface, where eye listen for you now,
light pure & simple as an echo of itself when it was fading fast,
the way out far beyond your memory, further still beyond
a doorway, perhaps, through which a lost fish swam once
looking for the way back to that baited hook it refused to bite, back
when the promise of light above this language was clear,
reflective, was shimmering like great music, or poetry,
before night came back washing everything away in darkness,
before they dredged up your once-shining face from that lake,
fish-eaten, bloated beyond even faith,

our hope a memory now eye have held onto all this time, love,
beyond even what the language of sound is to great music,

beyond even what metaphor is to this poem

SEPTEMBER 27, 2004

lunar moon eclipse over marfa, texas
one night—followed by a full orange
sun high in the blue the next morning—

between the marfa lights that sparkled
above the red-light tower,
                              down by the chinati mountains,
next to the mexican border, close to midnight,
the sky stretched wide as a black blanket
spread out on a king-sized bed
covered with pearls & diamonds,

behind us highway ninety cuts east
& west, snaking from van horn through marfa,
all the way to san antonio, on this evening
the highway is empty of lights of cars
& trucks, as the lunar eclipse bewitched us above

our mouths down here formed O's, amazed,
as a cool night breeze in marfa chilled
naked bodies of lovers elsewhere humping
their delicious thrills on soiled, rumpled sheets,

when its cold, sharp tongue of air
cut deep into their hot passion,

stilled their fervent ardor until another day

ST. LOUIS MUSIC FLASHBACK

they used to pack whatever clubs they played,
the musicians, always sharp as razor blades,
so hip, in fact, when they jumped clean
it meant something more than mere attitude,
though state of mind too was part of what they said
& wore when they mimicked the stance of homeboy
miles davis when he came home from the big apple to blow
his haunting golden horn, his eyes two hot
coals burning behind dark shades, his spirit
mesmerizing magnetized all eyes
in the club to where he stood, lean & mean,

in his stance he was a force field for all those
musicians who never left home, chose to stay behind
for whatever reason—a safe job
at the post office, a teacher, a wife & kids, old friends,
a mortgage on a house, car payments—
but it all boiled down to fear of leaving what they knew behind,
true security, was what albino red the great pianist embraced,
sam lazar, who burned it up on the hammond organ,
the quartet tres bien, all so beautiful, so afraid of what
unknown possibilities would bring them
outside their safe harbors—they couldn't risk failure,

so they locked up their dreams, threw away the keys,
lived vicariously through osmosis,
lived through the image of homeboy miles davis, became him—
the way he dressed, his attitude, his stance offstage,

his raspy speech after he busted his vocal chords,
his sweet, cool way of playing the music—

in fact in local clubs the people loved them for it
because miles *was* a god, absent his presence
what could they do between his visits
but settle for imitations of his stance,
pretend to be the true Prince of Darkness?

DIVA

again, for Dorothy Smith Marshall

my mother walks with certainty, ballerina-style,
she glides by up on the balls of her feet, tippy-toe,
her back straight as a plank of wood,
there is an air of haughtiness in her manner,
the way she looks at you is a command
about to happen, no doubt in what she says,
in her own mind she's already convinced herself
it's right, she's eighty-seven, a tiny woman,
when she's all made up, decked out in her finest clothes,
her arms, fingers, ears, & neck dripping jewelry,
she's regal in her bearing, but can blow warm & cold,
radiant when you catch her just right, in a good mood,
she will bless you with a bright beautiful smile
wide as daybreak, her laughter spraying light
mist all over you as when waterfalls hit rocks & liquid
bottom after dropping over a cliff, makes you think of music
entering your space with notes shimmy-shangling, but please
don't catch her wrong, say something rubbing sandpaper
rough up against her temperamental grain,
could be anything, large or small, everything changes,
her temper hisses, then explodes like a lit firecracker,
better pull back quick when her face clouds over,
her mood turns black as a day about to drop a tornado,
you better pull back quick before she flips her switch—
her once-warm eyes suddenly turn into twin smoldering
nuggets about to spit singeing fire all over you—
better turn back & go the other way, tout-de-suite,

before her verbal anger hits you like a category five
hurricane & you wonder how it all came to this
from this small, dainty, high-class looking,
proper woman with the ballerina style,
who just a heartbeat moment ago was flashing you
a soft, bright smile wide as daybreak, her laughter
spraying light sparkling bliss all over you,
made you think it was music entering your space,
made you think it was all light in this place

LUCILLE

for Lucille Clifton

if you were a guitar, lucille,
b.b. king would play beautiful blues
songs all over your ample spirit,

but you're a poet, sister,
so you play your own wondrous riffs
through notes of your honed words,

they dig down deep, sewn within
your music, boned, you keep them inside
your brief luminous sentences of echoes,

sounding like sonorous utterings,
flight seeking light inside a flute's breath,
bird wings lifting off on a wind's

rustling flight, your elliptic absences
pregnant with caesuras arrest us with their sorrow—
winged loves gone too fast from you now

always test the elixir of your rooted
deep faith, everywhere in your poetry
the conviction of living spirits, beauty

shining through the bravery of your life is
a bright, flashing beacon pulsating harmony
in all this darkness, your embrace

warm as the sun during summer,
it is abiding your faith that holds me fast to you
now, inside your sweet nourishing well of love

eye know there is a "river between us"
we can always cross over, we can
cross over it again & again & again,

can always cross over it with faith,
can always cross over it with love,
again & again & again,

like you do, lucille, like you do

THE SHOT

for Tiger Woods, at the 2005 Masters

we watched him loft a chip shot from the rough
on the 16th, the ball dropped from the sky
like an aspirin in the middle of the green,
then we saw it move right like pure magic,

like a basketball player pivoting
before making a deft move to the hole,

this spinning little white ball made a beeline
in the direction of the cup,
crawling over the green it had twenty-twenty vision,

everyone watched, held their breaths,
when it got to the lip of the cup it lingered,
trembled at the edge like it was afraid of heights,
before dropping like a ball of sugar
into a cup of black coffee,

then the crowd erupted as he kneeled,

then stood, ramming his balled fist into the sky,
celebrating having been blessed by a miracle
cameras caught him in his signature logo

& everyone knew then the rest was pure glory

FOR RICHARD PRYOR: 1940–2005

you danced on wing tips of raunchy humor, richard,
danced on edges of words flying high up in the blue(s),
you were the flight of so many birds soaring
toward freedom of expression, an idea clued you
in your in-the-pocket profane language, words mirroring
the jazzy tongue-lashing put-downs we blacks heard all
our screaming lives laughed out in barbershops, churches,
in beauty parlors, on street corners where gun-slinging local
black wordsmiths slapped down cruel, embarrassing all-comers
with their oral boasting toasts, so funny they leaned into caustic
hard verbal shootouts every day, sardonically hip they thrived
on cutting down to size all pretenders to their thrones
though none were even close to the genius you were in stand-up,
richard, you were the cat's meow, *the man* who had the gift
the quickest razor-tongue flashing under any & every sun
& everybody knew not to raise up & bother with your "dirty" words
words slicing clean to the bone in head-on comedic cutting sessions
& eye loved you when eye first heard you dishing it out on TV,
on records, you made everyone's hair stand up straight
with your machete-wielding stories rooted in peoria
eye knew you were the real deal throwing down *our* words
on stage, our african-american prometheus, fragile as you were
you had steel in your backbone, steel in your everyday
commitment to truth, flawed as you were too with drugs
so high you set yourself on fire, lived to tell about it
lived to laugh at the stupidity of yourself in self-deprecating
screaming routines, filled with truth, sadness, & hilarity
you are always with me, richard, & eye will judge
other comedians, how their words stand up next to yours

5.

MEXICAN LORE

for Aristco

we were on the road to see the monarch
butterfly "miracle" retreat in ocampo
& pass through the quaint little towns of dolores,
tzintzuntzan, named after hummingbirds,
the famous cemetery split in two there
by the new roadway & celebrated all over the world
on the day of the dead, sits on lake patzcuaro,
whose name imitates the sound
of flapping hummingbird wings,

when we stop for lunch, a kind-looking, short
mexican man, who likes my dreads tells me in american,
"mexican authorities circumcised Jesus
on january first," when eye ask him how he knows this,
the man smiled & said, "mexicans know everything
& if they don't know it they make it up"

THE WEST INDIAN DAY PARADE

for Leonard Fraser

if you want to jump up inside energy, cross over
from manhattan to brooklyn in september,
every year, on labor day, the west indian day carnival
parade jumps down eastern parkway
full of color, music, & pizzazz,

watch people waving flags of caribbean
nations—barbados, trinidad-tobago, st. lucia, haiti,
antigua, dominica, jamaica, st. kitts—
from behind police barricades, food scents draw us in,
tantalize the memory of nostrils,
for an instant the desire to return to homelands
focuses the need to vibrate the street with rhythms,
causes bodies to shake as if processed by spirits,

we watch gorgeous women agitate their bodies,
their stomachs rippling like airborne ribbons,
                                        or incoming sea waves,
match the oo-la-la up & down movement
of hottentot basketball bottoms, hips, & pelvises
humping coast to coast in a primeval frenzy,
as bands on floats pulsate native music thumping
inside their own rhythmic memory,

4 million revelers strong they jump up,
jump down, from eleven to dusk,
people from all races gawk at caribbean black

people of all shades, decked out in fabulous costumes
of gold, pink, blue, white, green, fuchsia,
orange, black, purple, brown, breasts firm as grape-
fruits burst from skimpy bikini cups, as revelers sport
headdresses full of indian feathers, women & men
splashed with sequins, gold dust, wearing spectacular beads,
gold & silver shoes, head scarves, bandanas—

some mimicking terrorist disguises that cover their faces
up to their eyes—a fashion statement? you go figure—

jump up, jump down, jump up, jump around,

as phalanxes of policemen make their presence known,
wear bored expressions on their faces—why do they look so
bored, with all this energy going on?

as the parade sashays down eastern parkway
crowds scream for their native floats, for the music they love
rooted in their memories, as cross-fertilized food odors
play succulent games with nostrils—
east indian, african, european, & asian flavors
mix ingredients chefs stir into mouthwatering mélanges—
drive stomachs crazy with desire, cause hunger
to raise up its head, as the body does in dance—

escovitch, pawpaw, & mango jam, curried goat,
callaloo, pepper pot, sauce ti malice, rice & peas,
biriani, fritters, rice & beans, polouri, boudin
creole, acra, jerk chicken, souse, langouste grillee,
stamp and go, sancocho, mango chutney, akee
& salt fish, pork roast calypso, meat patties,

as the parade winds down, the energy revs up
as the police lose control of the crowds
bursting at the seams, spilling over the barricades
people throw themselves out into the street to jump up
as the music boils, the men in blue throw up their hands
& some are seen even to shuffle their feet in time
with the rhythm, in sync with the flow,
cause nothing's going to happen
but a good time for all—& what's wrong with that
in this age of children being shot & blown up,
missiles & death everywhere we look—

what's wrong with jumping up, jumping down for a day,
what's wrong with watching people having a great time,

their faces bright as the dazzling sun on this day,

what's wrong, what's wrong with that?

CONNECTIONS

for Robert Antoni

1.

on a drop-dead clear day you took me down the waterway,
riding the miami river in your small motorboat, robert,
the skyline of miami backdropping our journey
                                        like on *miami vice,*
suddenly I was looking for a flock of pink flamingos skimming
low over biscayne's waves to burst into view, take over
the scene alongside don johnson & michael philip thomas
streaking by, squeezed into a wave-skipping cigarette boat,
front-end up, chasing drug-dealing "bad guys,"
but the scene was so tranquil here now as boats slid through oily,
dark, smelly, flotsam-filled waters on this november day
so different from the sparkling blue, pastel images
always surfeiting *miami vice* on celluloid,
with staccato gunfire blending with colors,
complete with rhythmic soundtracks & stunningly beautiful people
fused with all matter of races, dressed in linen,
wondrous bodies of women bursting from skimpy bikinis,
                        none of this was present this day, though the sky was
lovely as any eye have ever witnessed,
the mood—except for our laughter—was pensive
as we passed the venetian islands & san marco island
(where you used to live before barcelona, spain, robert, new york
city), silent now except for the sound of wet fish slapping
& flopping around metal pails after fishermen hauled them in
over concrete railings of the venetian causeway,

running low past islands of the same name,

spanning biscayne bay,

connecting miami beach to miami

& beyond here, out to the east the atlantic stretches
its foaming waves to touch the caribbean,

latin america, africa, & europe,

all these places blended inside you here, robert, where
your genes fuse genomes of all the modern world, your DNA
pumped through veins & arteries bright red
as your two-year-old son gabriel's vexed face, screaming now
at the top of his lungs, his innocent displeasure real,
contorts his beautiful face with roped veins
bulging from his temple & neck, his voice catching,

coughing, until you give him a drink,

then his transformation to calm is swift,
remarkable even, in the way his eyes laugh
with glee, now, as rubber car wheels squeal above us
over the causeway like scherzos, our laughter breaking,
skedaddling, shimmying through the air like skeins of yarn
skydiving from our mouths like musical notes

& we, too, robert, are like children, here in this world,
our blood fused within the nexus of history,
flowing within interconnecting musical tongues,
moving us—like this soiled river we are riding over now
is moving us—toward some secret rendezvous
we will discover when we get there

2.

what is the real meaning of any journey, mental surfing
through connections of our minds made real when we see,
at the end a possibility for redemption,
brought to life by what our eyes pick up along the way, we keep
information vital as blood pumped through our veins, is sacred
as heartbeats drumming through language as life-force,
glue, a synergy, perhaps, of oppositional music,
caught within the ebb & flow of sounds that each hears,
inside the moment, is close enough to rhythm, waterloo,
is beautiful enough to go there with ears & eyes wide open, too,
as to stand buffeted by a hurricane wind & crow,
"no wind exists anywhere like this but here," but how
would they know, having been nowhere else but here?

3.

nomenclatures of miasmas are sweeping the world,
oxygenating, they become looming specters of prophecy,
synergistic connections to the past,

if we pay attention to what connects us all, robert,
we might more easily move toward a real state of beauty,

move into a more blessed state of grace

IN SAINTE-ANNE, GUADELOUPE

for Jacques-Marie Basse and Derek Walcott

we wake to days in august bright with emerald
foliage shimmering around us,

        as if we were living in a lost paradise
somewhere, abundant with wild hummingbirds darting
through extravagant leaves, as orange flamboyance peek,
red hibiscus flowers dance high among the leaves,
as shining palm fronds wave like warrior sword blades,
lance through lush, whispering air heavy with heat,
sticky, even in the shade,

        as the ocean's murmuring bric-a-brac
is a low, constant reminder in the distance,
foaming to shore wave after wave terracing in,
one after the other, evokes memories of white pages
licked open by wind tonguing a book
left in the salt wash (it reminds me of history,
its far-flung journeys piling up here as sand eye wedge now
between my toes, next to the webbed imprints of birds,
the zigzagging trail of lizards wriggling through
the hieroglyphic ambrosia of amphibious ambivalence,
soaked in amber), just before the whispering goes

still, then, just as quickly, a fresh new breeze startles
with its coolness, licks a soothing tongue
wet across my sweating forehead,

blesses open my eyelids, weighed down now
with a gathering languor so heavy eye find myself drifting,
as in a dream, toward sleep,
nodding a herky-jerky head dance imitating a junkie's,
so pronounced at times my noggin resembles a cork
bobbing above a fisherman's line & hook,
                        after a hungry fish has bitten
& the struggle for its survival is on,

eye linger here for a moment, think of the breadfruit
leaves waving in benediction after the wind's blustering
command, rustling groves of mangoes & strawberries
just off the black snake of a road twisting through bouliqui
from sainte-anne, in central guadeloupe

& there, in bouliqui, the hibiscus are pink
buds imitating pursed lips waiting for a kiss,
while above birds lance close heavy air, plunge through amber
filigreed light between the lattice-drop of leaves
as the sun passes behind & over the treetops,
starting its daily descent toward the frigid pacific,
a sudden wet breeze startles my dreams with its here-
then-gone sweet tongue of my wife's cool breathing,

then, back in sainte-anne, wrenched out of my dreams,
eye watch dragonflies swim the air
sweating toward twilight, while white butterflies wobble,
float like tiny sacred ghosts between the scarlet, yellow
flamboyance, the emerald leaves holding the hibiscus's
red lips, deep within our own paradise here

at auberge le grande large,

among the lengthening shadows, palm fronds waving
like servants above a giant frog, who seems to be leading
a deafening choir of other toads in a symphonic offering,

eye listen in awe as nature's orchestra boggles my senses
once more with its beautiful perfect pitch & rhythm

A WOMAN IN THE WATER

eye see a woman in the caribbean sea-
water off the beach of ste. anne,
she is walking with curlers in her nappy hair,
a pink net, a straw hat on top like a crown,
she is black, walking through the sea,
the sun is high in the vaulting blue,
she is humming a beautiful tune,
the sea is clear light green to its sandy bottom,
as some cats' eyes are green, some striking women,
the water is warm as a freshly drawn bath,
the woman's tune is so beautiful
eye want to know the meaning
under the words married to the rhythm
there, inside the song, a feeling of joy
eye hear in her deep voice walking
through the sea there, wearing a red dress,
the water is warm & clear & light green
as a cat's eye, those of a striking woman,
all the way down to their sandy bottom

A KITE ABOVE THE BEACH

coconut leaves shiver, wave, dance, green-golden, stream
like manes of flaxen hair behind galloping racehorses,
high above auberge le grande large, in sainte-anne,
pulsating voices of croaking frogs, buzzing crickets swell below
the gathering darkness, yeasts like bread, just before night falls,
raises a winking, full moon—a one-eyed cat's view—
a cyclops looking at the world, just before lights click on,
headlamps of cars pop bright into view, before twin lanterns
guiding two watchmen on their rounds, a lone, fragile kite trailing
a snaking train of trembling ribbons, flutters skyward, a speckle
above the beach, a hint of uncertainty there, like a young bird
searching for its mother before climbing upward toward curiosity,
riding a lifting alizé might climb further than perhaps
its mother taught it to fly, now its ascent hints a fretful hesitation
just being up there, higher than it's ever gone before, suddenly
a gut-wrenching fear of the unknown seems to consume it,
like a beginning swimmer being pulled farther & farther out to sea,
right before a freezing panic sets in, grips him, like now, like this
young bird, this fragile, drifting kite fluttering ever upward
before darkness swallows them with its daunting black magic,
here full of sounds, sea waves washing in hissing & foaming,
voices of people, frogs, & crickets fusing their orchestral miracle
& a full moon up there, in the night sky, staring like a cyclops—
a one-eyed black cat looking down on all this teeming planet

THE MOON IS A LEMON WEDGE

the moon is a lemon wedge over guadeloupe
in the night sky, its likeness swims bold
inside a cold, tall glass of rum & coke
standing on a table, on a white veranda wrapped
around an airy home somewhere around high noon,
on a bright, clear day, somewhere in sainte-anne,
as flamboyance bloom orange, high up,
or low-down in shimmering, lush green leaves,
beneath the sun's wicked eye, in a blue sky paraded by clouds
soft as cotton candy riding over forms of swimmers in emerald
warm caribbean waters, but you are not there
except in your poetic imagination, but here, under this
starlit sky, right now, in all this blooming darkness,
driving the back roads of grande terre, on a clear night
& looming the moon is a lemon wedge suspended
above you, a still life in an artist's paint-splattered room,
a beacon wedge lodged inside a lover's dreaming bloom,
a milky-blind eye of ray charles, or stevie wonder

SOMETIMES IN MONTEBELLO

rain storms come swooping in wearing veils of dancing
mist, come whooshing in over guadeloupe with a switching,
swishing motion of women's skirts when they swing
wondrous hips, as probing tongues of scandalous winds,
who, if truth be told, are nothing more than peeping gigolos
prancing around, lifting dresses with the sweet,
whispering sounds of their breezy tongues, they are lyrical,
these winds, fleet, sometimes, soft as scented talcum
caressing skin with soothing touches, these rains
murmuring secret lullabies rustling through leaves,
bending tips of grass with fingers curling softly around
them as if they were follicles of a lover's hair,

eye watch veils of rain wash over the green body
of a lizard as it darts through luminous grass quick as fear
when it drops down on you & you run lickety-split
into the unknown, suddenly eye become the lizard
running for cover when lightning strikes,
zigzags across a sky gone black as miles davis's skin,
his smile a sliver of moon in the distance where clouds break,
the sea murmuring secrets beneath them now
is foaming waves of histories fish know but will not tell us
until their flopping or still deaths appear floating before us
bloated, reveal the poison inside their spirits
they could not tell us of when alive, now
they are washed over by cascades of foaming music,
polluted waves sweeping the greed of men, filled with blues
they always forget, just ask dick cheney, george bush,

ask them if they know ajoupa blues coursing through
sad raging eyes of people before us now in iraq, haiti,

ask these men if they know anything other than greed,
power, if they have ever taken time to understand
the beauty of rains sweeping in wearing veils of dancing mist,
fanning out, whooshing across the imagination, the magic
singing in the swishing sounds of a woman's skirt,
those marvelous hips switching back & forth,

just ask dick cheney, george bush, men like these
if they know the deep secrets of a deep, human love,

ask them if they understand the history of blues & rain

THE OLD BLACK MAN WALKING

the old black man walking montebello road,
swinging a rusted machete seems angry
as he chops off heads of flowers,
                              perhaps he's thinking

this flora represents heads of french government officials
he sees oppressing him, black bourgeoisie stand-ins
on the island for the long, machiavellian
                                        arm of france,

perhaps he is just a simmering image of anger
now, at everything surrounding him he can't control
in this new world of computers, globalization,

where he doesn't fit in, who knows what triggers
the whys & where-fores, the fire igniting a fuse

EYE AM THINKING OF MOMENTS

eye am thinking of moments when my thoughts run
free as twisting wild vines growing under the sun,
soft rain gathering new puddles around roots,
dewdrops of crystal on flower petals, mist swelling
in the air, the sound of language percolating everywhere,
music, the hum of creation improvising rhythms,
mysterious as soukougnans shedding human skin,
throwing off light, magic comes when you least expect it,
is a lewoz of drums, pippiree birds serenading, colibris eating
bananas, gwo kas speaking in seven-rhythms time, bonda-butts
responding to deep ancestral memories, a dirge
becomes a kite, is a beautiful sight up there flying
free until a strong wind comes, breaks it apart,

like syllables of poems gone wrong, surfers on waves,
the mind miscalculates the power of rhythm,
the deep notion all things have, memories of their own magic,
to change directions, as when volcanoes explode, floods
take back space where fingers of its rivers once ran,
where water first came from, is as mysterious
as why tornadoes, hurricanes swirl across time, space, creating
conditions for their own destructive artistry, heard in the syllables
their winds bring, is a certain clarity inside their own savage beauty,
an indelible music in the ferocious howling gusts of rhythmic voices
screaming frightening secrets throughout their lifetimes,
everywhere either of them passes dreams of men flung
stunned into air, where they fly like beats of drums,

what do we know of ancient secrets, magic, pippiree birds
singing in the sweet, gathering sounds of evening,
bwa-kabritt crickets, large as small boulders screeching loud
as some scary, imagined zombies flying through the night
to bring us ancient cries predicting rain, sounding mating calls,
they land high up in leafy branches, on rooftops,
surrounded by darkness, what do we know, those of us blah-blah
in violent, industrial cities, living on the run, zooming around
like bats out of hell, or crawling around our steel-encased homes,
gridlocked on freeways like shoppers on a sale day at the mall,
or underground in subways smelling of pee, oil, & metal,
what do we know of mofwazés, soukougnans shedding skin,
throwing off light, pippiree birds singing sweet love,
songs of gwo-ka drums gathering lewoz rhythms,

magic can come when you least expect it, from anywhere,
mysterious as the source of hurricanes, tornadoes, language
in the air percolates everywhere, music, like mist, suddenly there,
swelling here, blooming fresh as new flowers after soft rain drums
bonda-butts into the air responding to ancestral memories,

climbing from the earth, through the body, like duende
climbing from the earth, through the body, like duende

WE HAVE COME HERE AGAIN

for Margaret & for our friends Maryse, Richard, Luc, & Micheline

we have come here again to hear the talking drum of our galvanize
rooftop beaten with hands & feet of falling raindrops
speaking to us here, inside rhythms, to listen to choirs of leaves
whispering secrets outside our wide-open windows & doors,
speaking a language bringing the world outside inside to live with us,
is close to paradise on this earth filled with terror,
as a swirling wind sluicing through all openings probes each
& every corner of our little house here, searching like snakeheads,
feverish tongues of heat-stricken lovers circling inside each other's
mouths, right before their twin orgasms explode, together,
right before a gray day turns green in montebello
& hummingbirds preen in whirs of spinning wings, hesitate,
stop in midflight, like tiny helicopters in front of ylang-ylang flowers,
drink the sweet fuel-nectar with nozzle-beaks,
then dart away clean into massive clusters of green leaves,
shadows serving as hiding places ripple under deep cover,

below, eye wait for the sun to break through with laughter,
wait for blue to crack open clouds like a can opener,
to lighten up the sea's lingering gray frown on the water's surface,
wait for the aqua-green palette of waves to be burnished clean & glow
with the sun's clearing focus, so eyes of all of us swimming here
can see through saltwater from top to bottom,
sand shifting gently beneath our feet, from bottom up,
the water soothing my toes, clear as a church bell ringing slow
in sainte-anne's square is lucid on sundays, the air fresh with lemon
smells, mangoes, pregnant with people speaking salt-&-pepper

creole, their breaths laced with scents of ti punch—rum mixed
with sugar, lime, or gingembre—counterpunch each other,
their boxing styles depending on what class or color strata
they're in, a different rhythmic code embedded
inside the tongue's DNA, is a microscopic chip
recognizing, or rejecting tonal shifts, nuances,

so margaret & eye wait here, outside of it all, familiar strangers
as we are inside our own country, friendly ghosts
passing through these moments with people refusing to fuse with us,
or themselves, for that matter, the *other* inside everyone here, too,
always in front of us, as here, or there, it doesn't matter,
though here the moments are still beautiful, calm,
we are inside a wondrous flora, brilliant with lavish colors,
as is this beautiful mix of jambalaya races stirred together,
though beauty is in the eyes of the beholder, here,
as elsewhere, we move through rhythms knowing the key
to tongues swapping spit is love, the passion of language, music,
reaching out to convert ears to listen to sweet, strange
rhythms deep down inside, is familiar as great art is, is a dance
step coming through the night's tongue carrying secrets, love,

is familiar as heartbeats, familiar as drumbeats of rain-
rhythms on rooftops, choirs of leaves whispering ancient secrets
outside windows & doors, clouds riding swift wind currents high
above, threatening or softening throughout the day, like history
when it moves at the churning speed of a gathering hurricane,
or caresses the moment with a licking lover's tongue,
carries a sweet soft beauty some never understand

6.

MUSIC IS LANGUAGE

when you hear the wind warbling through trees,

like choirs, beam-eyed children descanting
above the melody of whistling air,
church bells ringing is language dancing,

everywhere,

words breaking across playgrounds like tiny feet
prancing, pebbles skipping over the wet face of a lake
                                        is hearing language as music,

when you hear children playing hide & go seek,
listen, when you hear lonely dogs barking, cats meowing
        in the dark hours,

                                wolves howling at the moon, birds trilling
at daybreak, when the sun climbs high in the blue
                        in the east, it reminds of a gold coin
flipped & spinning in the air like a note,

when you hear & see things surrounding you like this,

then you know everything in the world speaks a language,
know everything in the world can be music,
even leaves in trees sawed by breezes remind ears
of violin strings singing in a symphony,

they evoke colors, music is a kind of sonorous language
speaking sometimes in orotund-rhythms heard by eyes,
a kind of sound-tongue the colors black or white call to mind,
what sound the colors red, yellow, or brown sing to ears,
the music of love, hatred, beauty, water falling, laughter,

butterflies fluttering, birds diving & swooping, rainbows,
what sound do you hear when small hands clap together,
when eyes laugh, cars skid & crash & blood flows

as a crimson river, before transforming itself,
becomes branching fingers of a clawing hand, rivulets,

everywhere is music, all of it language,

the rat-tat-tat of words hiccupping like rap,
hip-hop-ping across air,

is sound syncopating

& everywhere we hear music as language,

trumpets & saxophones blaring,
guitars strumming, everywhere is music,

is language in the air, with a flair,

everywhere is music, music everywhere

WHAT IS IT POETRY SEEKS

what does poetry seek beyond
turning a phrase, or two,
cutting a figure of speech with a word
sharp as a shaver's wish
to rid the face of hair,
       slicing through the tangle of texts
as a razor blade would lopping off

an ear, a way of hearing,

what is the path pruning takes
in revision when it cuts back unconscious
flows inside language
the way lava flows edit themselves, perhaps
in a manner a tree trimmer goes about
eliminating dead leaves,

on the other hand winds

become a kind of reordering
inside fury of a storm, is a form,
perhaps, like the way a poet rewrites a poem,
a painter re-imagines a canvas,
a musician re-invents a solo,
a politician changing what they meant
right before our disbelieving eyes,

is a constant re-invention,

is all of us during daily reshaping of meaning,
is language always in search of itself,
new ways to express the moment,
                         to create freedom
in an instant, like a bird or a trane moving through
sound in real space, in real time,
like picasso or al loving
with an eye, a brush, or a splotch of color
re-creating a moment through an image,

a feeling in an instant is a changing of the guard,

eye tell you, metaphor is a way of hearing, seeing
things, being in the moment, in real time,

right here, right now

WHAT IS IT

what is it we come to know through poetry, music,
through language stitched with images, colors,
syntax stretched into movement,
metaphors deepening layer after layer, sentences
laced with symbols that connect us, or disconnect us,
one to another, through figurative speech, sound
rooted inside meaning, spirit, rhythm,
a deep measure of how close we are truly bonded,
no matter how violence seems to break apart
dreams, is perhaps a signal raising its head,
an answer inside mixed metaphors,
a broken rhythm leading the way to whatever is out there
singing for us, to us, the moment—a breath of freshness arriving—
here & now, in this movement of syllables
tell us what we always knew ourselves to be,
thought inside our own visions,
knew through language shaped out of music, echoes,
the way we speak to each other through gestures,
speak to moments of love through tongues

SWITCHIN' IN THE KITCHEN
AFTER AN ART SHOW OF THE SAME NAME
BY MILDRED HOWARD

rhythms be switchin' in kitchens when cooks work magic
through pots, out on dance floors hips gyrate
like poets constructing lines sometimes switch & drop
from proper to colloquial, new days are forever changing color,
weather, voices switch back & forth in the sky,
down here breezes caress bodies, sashay through thoroughfares,
inside language doing whatever flip-flops it has to

to survive, inside music everything matters, a poet steps off
the count syncopating syllables, meters, the voice-music falls
over the edge of a cliff of chromatic scales, shades splash bright clues
as water skedaddling new diamond-drops imitates flushed birds
spraying syllables through showering waterfalls, mist,
skeining language skews, stretches, slips & slides through
space, sounds crack ensconced rapture somewhere here, listen
to these hairsplitting ruptures politicians spew every day
in sad convergences of bad, flat notes,

as time signatures skip-to-my-loo through lace
grace notes bloom in poetic lines, loom posthaste, push
& zing the voice through sound, shimmy-shingle,
juxtapose in place the poet's high-energy gymnastics, highjacked
words switch up in double-backs, pivots, crossovers,
as skywalkers wing word-plays deep beyond boundary lines,
where NBA gunners drop trays, pop cords, create balladic
touchés, body-magic up inside rhyme schemes rhapsodic,

their body music reflects light as spirits lance curling through
prismatic flight, oh, tell me about it air jordan, kobe bryant, lebron
james, up there in the lights imitating bird, bebop, well
you needn't, because great solos are tracer-bullet flights, sun ra
& coltrane breathing as they zoom riding high-priest monk riffs
into any rooms they played, brought high-jinks-magic for poets
to play, eye put a little bloom on this poetic language-tip, riff
diglossic, scatology, piss-zoom in on a neo-logic trip, rapology
dripping words of obfuscation, filo-plumes, orgasmic dolos,
zip through traces of fizz on the rebound of a champagne bliss,
eye telescope hubble inside flues, constantly scope bubbles, link
strings of pearls inside champagne glasses, sans clues,
my attitude fed by gas rises to the top, floats over blown grass,
grows like sassafras, my voice a reverberating echo
inside a memory dome, communicate with my mother,
break through the fog of old-age disconnect, eye ask you now brotha,
where's your boom box, are your false teeth lost in a jar somewhere,
is your ego drowning inside an old piss pot, funky as this sick war
invented by chicken-hawk cheney-bush-wags, rumsfeld

& is this an early morning alarm clock going off for you,
sans hard-on, a wake-up call, a tall drink of confusion,
are you a two-watt on a dimmer-switch belching gas ignorant as snuff,
a moron looking for conundrum, inside a bait & switch pimp niche,

but don't panic just yet, run out to investigate chromatography,
lapis lazuli, do you really think you might need a tad bit of viagra
to get your love-thang juiced out on the dance floor,

as you're listening to an echo-chamber of words, what
was that reverb glancing off those winged syllables that flew by,

birds inside a sentence laced with miles & miles of blue history,
stitched with trumpet blasts, obbligatos, obdurate
against past abracadabras, running like doodly squats,
who only drop dimes on the rhythmic line,
while some only drop dimes behind set screens,

which one are you, mr. flip-flop, slow on the crossover,
"switchin' in the kitchen" is what eye mean to do here,

this poem's trying to do a dance on this page with words,
metaphor & reverb, switchin' back & forth through rhythm & time
signatures, improvising through space, switchin' up on a dime,
my lines trace words looking for birds winging through dirges
blue as lady day's words on "strange fruit,"

sluicing through language, this poem's tracer-bullet tip
tries to put hip bloom on the rapolic verbal trip,
pigology, filo-plumes, fusing words to create a new syntax
with no nonsense from politically correct verbs to slice & dice,
string out a proper poetic sentence, solo, hello,
my voice shooting through syntax quick as a string of escaping
bunny rabbits, looking for a way out of a house of glass,
rising to the top like a linkage of pearl-drop bubbles,

eye jazz sassafras, telescope hubble-constantly

inside the galaxy, eye raise a champagne glass,
offer up razzmatazz, rhythms carving out

meaning inside language, images that might last

7.

THE ARCHITECTURE OF LANGUAGE

for Allan Kornblum, Carolyn Holbrook, Lois Vossen, Christopher Janney, & Al Loving

1.

the wind swirling through the blueprint of speech,
bare bones of utterances found wrapped there
inside sound, a language, history
      stitching itself together, where bodies wrap themselves up
inside measures, reinvent syllables,
sprout wings, where voices lifted up by spirits
           hurl themselves
                  into singing, echoes,

as a man with a drooping handlebar mustache slaps down
a hard black domino bone-white with stars
embedded in the night of its color,
its shape & form square
           stares up from its hard skin of black ivory,

as another man lights a fire under he said-she said innuendo,
his constant bantering setting up rules of the game,
the way it will play itself out
when the playing field is slanted toward the speaker,
his words controlling the flow

inside the subliminal seduction of sentences,
where language can become anything, mixing words,
mata hari shots of heroin manipulating the brain
during a first sweet moment of celebration,

just when you thought you had pulled everything back together
again, in that first moment of half-light just when you thought
the words you heard singing could possibly become
the very wind you always needed to lift your spirit
up into flight, to hear a music that was always there,
always possible, but somewhere hidden outside
your comprehension, its chords encoded
in mystery but there all the while chasing invention,
magic, now & forever, a breathtaking moment hovering
over shimmering blue water rippling with waves, intensity
& heat, a line of words sizzling with ingredients of jambalaya,
foo-foo, cooked like a clifford brown solo, was replete,
ingress was possible there through which words could flow
to point a fractured finger of an archipelago out to sea,
to show where the great poetic muse of wind might build
a scaffolding from rhythms, stacked up from word plays, puns,
jokes, caesuras, enjambments, fused in a burst of language,
flight, in the first cracked moment of daylight,
when the moon has slipped back undercover
& the sun begins to blow out its hougan's breath
of fire tempered by distance, calibrated by a man high up
inside the blue skies of his imagination,
inside the heat of creation, deep in song, a man who could be
you, could be me, could be a woman emitting a high sharp cry
shrill inside a call of divination, worship

beneath these words a street of boiling tar way down deep
stretches out now as a track for this poem
sizzling like a ribbon of asphalt at high noon in phoenix,
burns flesh like lava flows in hawaii

in the dog-day's heat, microwave oven of august,

where fat earthworms fry crisp to black wing tips on pavement
where they pause, looking like detached stingers
of scorpions, replicas of fishhooking commas arresting words
inside clauses, shaping the ultimate breath of our sentences,
speech oscillates here like winking membranes,
quick as tongues flicking liquid fire down scorched throats,
lye of incendiary words flaming hot as wind-driven forest fires
in california, burning leaves dropping from branches
like faces in nazi ovens, melt from memory,
like days burned from calendars,
as the pages of our lives are numbered here
where we stand up or fall down, ears wagging heads
full of blues inside the sound musicians spawn
inside test tubes today, where our speech becomes
                                    hissing snake tongues
outside our heads, words flicking fast as popping sparks
from the snapped off-end of an electrical wire tip,
after a storm dropped its coiled tail into a pool of charged water
& is (yes) like a snake's body (well) shaping itself into an O
or a cowboy's rope looping itself (yes) into another O
                              like the shape of a dead man's mouth
after sucking down or blowing out his last breath
(well, yes) is like a black hole there

in space (another O)

could be an apparition of fakery
could be an apparition of skullduggery
could be an apparition of organic metaphysics
                              political theater

could be an apparition of hiccupping drudgery
could be a demigod of miasmas, holocausts
could be a holy shaman leading to song
& is its own particular kind of passageway to language
filling up the blooming opening of that place
with its own music, its own kind of mysterious magic, a space,
a language filled with ambiguities of silence,
sound buried deep there like light during midnight hours,

a paradox, silence, as in death there is always
the living breath lurking somewhere in a song

2.

sometimes new language is a storm dropping songs,
suddenly from some secret place high up
inside a swirling system of weather—
itself an ever-changing code of utterances—
it communicates the alchemy of nature when it appears
assembled by God's mad architects of sound
it explodes new rhythms out into the open in a whirling,
cacophony of calamitous syllables
full of mysterious soundscapes, lightning bolts shattering
the moment, unzipping dark clouds clothing the sky,
rips it into veined fissures of an old woman's legs,
reveals an elephant trunk of spinning winds howling
in the half-light as it drops down, it evokes in me
moaning voices of ancestors thrown overboard
during the middle passage,

it is a scaffolding of tongues we hear crisscrossed
with different rhythms & cadences, meters,
forms from which newly found structures of poetry are created,
we hear birthed & sprung into the air there fresh music
mimicking today's speech, mirroring thirsty syncopation, sound
cross-thatched with distinctive cultural DNA seduces voice
through poetic architectonics of lingua franca,
architraves of crossbeam sentences lay themselves
floor by floor, build new structures of language that speak
to us, who intersect at crossroads everywhere

3.

kind of blue in green miles music sings to us
inside the ether flow, sounds as alphabets blow mean
solos high above cumuli, a language of silent dreams
flows through darkness with speed & longing, embraces
light spreading across a pregnant sky, through cracked lips
of morning, a voice heard imitating a flute
where clouds bloom their heads like pop-up ghosts,
yeast through long segues between black & blue intervals,
down below, blowflies torch another pregnant pause,
deepens the space between ahmad jamal & clueless doodoos,
between "lady day" & test-tube imitators
the memory chip of voice richness is lost somewhere in between
the two, replaced by marketing frenzy
because of cleavage & greed, eye ask what greatness is lost here,
what should we remember when speaking of imitation
in the name of song, comparing it to the real thing,
                              what made american music great

was not physical beauty enhanced by breasts bouncing through air,
not platinum/gold teeth flashing, doo-rags,
but pure voice/genius making music in blues, jazz, country
& western, rock 'n' roll, gospel, rhythm 'n' blues, bluegrass,
rap, classical, all beautiful when deep richness is there,

tradition is innovated deep in the grain, beyond image,
beyond the cloning sameness of musak,

is a language communicating with people everywhere
intersecting at crossroads throughout the world,

4.

at 116th street & 7th avenue in harlem,
english mixes with french & wolof, pops
like senegalese talking drums, impregnates bootylicious air
with rap-rhythmic speech scatting out on the streets
where new voices mack the juba-rattle of flying hands down,
slap tightly strung skins, mix jambalaya riffs into flow
caca flow inside rhapsodic rapology,
clock new inventions scratched across grooved tongues
spinning & springing from vinyl,

bodies breakdancing across airwaves like syllables
track trends coast to coast, cross international boundaries, rap
new-wave crack language-beats, seduce hearts & cultures
as architectonic magic fuses clues inside colloquial rhythms,
harp everyday popular speech, everywhere bringing the news
as everything is changing in this very moment,

everything is changing everywhere poetry grows
word by word, sound by sound, form by form, cadence by cadence,
mack by mack, word plays sluicing under the syllables
stitching evolving language into innovative soundtracks,
found in the very air we breathe every day

everywhere, everything is changing

5.

each new day begins with the sun rising after night
swooped down with a black cape full of stars
& moonlight shining like diamonds left in the afterglow,
but it all passes, is cyclic, things change again & again
like poetry, it's normal the way the world reorders itself
time & again the highs become lows, systems
destroy themselves, it is the nature of things,

when night becomes day moments are viewed, flashed
in & through a different light

architectural structures are altered,
their language full of shifting metaphors in the slinking
half-light, new rhythms replace old ones,
music is syncopated with improvisational modes, moto-flows
push aside goose-stepping syllabic metronomes
stomping through time & space on white pages, in speech
when spoken in entombed air it echoes,
sometimes fractures inside the ear,

surprise happens every day, different colors mix
inside speech, a jambalaya-paella fused speech complete
with fruits of the sea, clacking chickens, stomach sounds
full of rice & bean palava feijoada gumbo speak,
it is the natural way to create new cuisine, poetry, music,

mooing cows, woo-wooing owls, lyrical birds, the winds'
natural syllables rolling from fluted mouths in spring, summer,
whispered softly as a lyrical caressing breath seductive
as a lover's sweet undulating tongue,

they enter the world, become a new way of hearing/speaking,
everything changes, the way we hear
sounds we never heard, never paid attention to,
everything changes, the way we hear,
see & know things from different angles,
                              everything changes,

                    like new architecture rising into the blue

as glass & steel fingers pointing up to where
religion swears God is—is the Spirit really there?—

                              everything changes,

it is normal to be afraid of the unknown,

normal as cracked mirrors throwing back changes our faces see
every day we look into them as we grow older
                              everything changes,

day changes to night the sun replaces the moon
it is normal the way our world turns every day
on its axle like a roulette wheel spinning
our lives, our fates locked in the luck of the draw,
the spoke-gears driving the wheels of a speeding car
losing control on a black highway slick with ice,
the throw of the dice at a gambling table
is what this poem seeks to express through voice

6.

the pure voice is heard best in solitude, silence, like when
eye watch a small crab enter a dark hole
in damp mud in deshaies, guadeloupe, at taino village
cottages looking over the beach & waves of a blue-green
caribbean sea, later in the distance gwo ka
drummers crack night's stillness with rhythmic genius, machete
chops of their flying hands slap tightly-drawn skins, track sounds
seldom heard in america, their voices
mixing with brilliant orchestral scores of crickets
improvising with voices of tiny frogs, wind-tongue speaks
wet with salt off the caribbean as bats dive low through trees,
the droning threat of a humming dengue mosquito
can be heard, poised to strike, suck blood from me
equal to its own weight, but eye smash the threat
before it becomes real, leaving a mangled
blood-spot trembling on my skin,

when day breaks again the miracle of deshaies rises,
black hummingbirds stop on a dime in flight

drink nectar from a flower, their beating wings a blur,
transcendent choirs of birds serenade in this place
wondrous as ladera resort between the pitons

                              in st. lucia to the south,

as the sun sets, darkness swoops down again
an ancient shaman unfurling a black cape of mystery
full of diamonds we call moon & stars, bats dive
here again slicing through shadowed latticework of leaves
like fighter jets, they give off weird shrill cries,
it is a kind of poetry, a different music
my ears adjust to listening for its rhythms,
alert for any surprises bat voices might bring

7.

with their musical rhythm, structure, idioms slip through air
into fragments of speech in flight throughout the world,
light up the night inside refracted air,
organize themselves from improvisation into sentences,
sluice through our ears like laser beams, musical
chords & notes chewed off spitting syllables
shot like bullets from young mouths to explode inside our ears,
shape breath through songs of griots, the lives of people
whose voices build block by block from call & response
antiphonal neologic constructs,
like sunday morning preacher's throwing down hoodoo
                              architectonic-juju, DNA inventions boogalooing,
shaping the gospel, those churchified hallelujahs, mixing
boogie-woogie doodoo sounds cruising through street cadences,

rolling off soothsayer's blistered tongues,
as light glances off their platinum/gold teeth—razor blades?—
like sun rays bouncing off insect-looking mirrored windows squared
in sleek skyscrapers stabbing through polluted air like stilettos
throughout mestizo cities of the postmodern globe,

everywhere this architectonic-juju creates new metaphors
inside musical sounds blending fresh articulations, mix,
moto-cell phones ringing in bathrooms, showers,
hang from their own hooks

                                    voices entering the digital age,
sashay through a maze of computers,
download into iPods hip-hopping the globe,

this poem articulates a language seldom heard
in the mummified academies filled with tweedy gatekeepers,
tight-mouthed rejection stretched across their wire-thin lips,

                                    unable to hear wondrous music
swelling through the air, unable to dance in celebration,
their bones refusing all movement,
unable to recognize any language other than their own
metallic goose-stepping military rigor, their flat-footed sentences
straight as lines on EKG screens

no mellifluous magic, no syncopation, no surprise
there, no improvisation,
but close-minded poetry mirroring ethnophobia,
decrepit with deep fear

& claustrophobia replacing light

8.

this poem calls for a poetry of openness in america, now,
where voices skedaddle through time & space,
signatures riffing, creating on the margins,
screeching like cats at a cutting session, out on a fence,
like bird & monk up at minton's in harlem,
playing music like they owned it, like mahalia jackson,
leontyne price, willie nelson, johnny cash, chuck berry, aretha
franklin, the beatles, los lobos, u2 & bono,

will grow from voices of whitman, paz, neruda, márquez, hughes,
walcott, baraka, brooks, ellison, shange, rich, cesaire, or cruz
(riffing on the language we hear in our hearts & ears
is a new way of hearing & listening)

the american voice is not white or black, european or asian,
middle eastern or african, but mestizo, fused with jambalaya
palava feijoada gumbo, it speaks a musical language
bewitching our ears with what grows from a collective linguistic
flow, is a fusion of new syllabic magic rolling off the tongue
in a mélange of rhythmic sounds,
like la cucaracha is more syncopated than roach or bug,
(means the same thing, but is a dancing word
full of power)—can you say, la cucaracha!
can you hear power in language flow as beautiful, spiritual,
the pulse of being in the moment instead of the past,
on time instead of behind time,
feeling the breath of wind in your face can last
as it happens, like music tracking heartbeats pumping
in your own chest right now is a flow

9.

great language is a shower of words inside a blizzard
of tongues full of rhythms & syllables, is a flow,
is snowstorms of meaning coming & going everywhere our ears
turn, hear rainstorms, tornadoes, lightning bolts unzipping clouds
towering around the calm, savage eye of hurricanes, is a flow
coming & going, bringing new systems of music,
new ways of listening connected to hearing,
structures carrying a host of evolving languages, roiling tongues
inside cross-fertilized speech of immigrants & new poetry,
is a flow also located in the evil eye of katrina, rita
swirling in from the gulf of mexico carrying thunder & death,
foaming with cataclysmic omens, terrors beyond any understanding,
categories beyond any knowing what horror will bring

through cracks of daylight destruction unfolding, rancid bodies
bloated, floating in toxic water, is a language, is a flow
                                 we hear but do not know how to recognize

thirty-foot storm surges speaking in tongues more violent
than any language we think we hear or know,

is a flow disjunctive beyond any application of money,
is perhaps a cosmic spiritual payback
for bug-eyed children who mirror the language of hunger,
murder, no sympathy, or empathy for blues people festering
in a place full of heat, water, mosquitoes, poisonous snakes,
high prices for gasoline for cars thirsty for petro, is a flow
of anarchy spreading like a plague in this place, is a form of language
ignited by category-five winds & angry seawater foaming salt
& screaming in the voodoo language of the sea goddess, erzulie,

hougans blowing calamities ashore through their mouths
of long bamboo horns, is perhaps a payback
for all the terrors released in this flow

when coffins, mummified corpses, leering skeletal bones
unearthed by katrina's savage flooding tongue
are scattered like dead leaves & broken branches all over
louisiana's devastated countryside, it tracks the fall posthaste
of america's once promise of greatness,
lost here in this macabre jumble of unknown spirits
evicted from their graves with no names, identity,
no race-ticket or skin color has privilege in this space
of spirits displaced, scattered from former resting places
of chipped tombstones—also scattered—
their skulls reminding us of broken teeth of ex-fighters, junkies,
these corpses grinning teeth set in jaws of cracked bone,

is a powerful language screaming for redemption,
if we look deeply into this moment it reveals our true selves
in these spaces we live in corrupted by greed,
skin color, class, religion, power at all cost,
                                        is a definite language
suffocating in claustrophobia, ethnophobia, no connection
to the real world, to the flow (caca) growth of humane language,
poetry inside the most profound beauty of utterance
sings still inside the deepest grain of that flowering word,

sound by sound, word by word, speech evolves into beautiful
architecture, creates a scaffolding of cross-fertilized utterances
crossbeamed inside poetic sentences fused with music,
where metaphors spring from deepest sources of community,

these are the seeds that will link, bond us together

10.

after tongues of fierce winds howl full of calamitous journeys,
shipwrecked adventures swept astray by circular history,
where are we going, feeble question marks of human embryos
bloating after the wind's anger has died down, turned soft & gentle
as a sweet tongue of breeze caressing the passion of naked lovers,
where are we going led by troglodytes in dark suits selling wolf
tickets, tiny metal flags festooning their lapels,
violent little chicken-hawk men in seats of power,

where are we going rerunning all this bric-a-brac fear of hitler's
germany, murmuring a language full of evil secrets, murder,
mysterious as the ocean's salty sandpaper tongue of screeching
felines carrying sounds evoking warnings,
where are we going on this stormy sea full of huge treacherous rocks,
100-foot waves looming toss our premonitions like matchsticks,
thunderclaps of vowels flooding the peaceful conversations
we try to evoke within a spiritual connection,
where are we going carrying this toxic speech full of static
buzzing like hornets or flies through this pestilential
space where we live out our lives full of fear,
trepidation, & hateful loathing,
where are we going on this stormy sea,
heading into a space full of huge sharp rocks,
behind time instead of on time,

where are we going, going, going

11.

thunderclaps of vowels, raging rivers flooding
conversations, carrying languages, coming & going,
as the wind blows a mango out of a tree it speaks, too,
the moment it hits the ground, in the future there will be
new sounds when buzzing flies start feasting on
the mango's sweet nectar as its flesh rots away,
sinks into a swarm of feverish maggots,
is a kind of language whispering close to silence,

speaking inside this moment, it marks an instant
inside time, like musicians or poets riding the rhythms of wind,
the ocean's improvisational breath of misty saltwater, now
catapulting a fish into the sky, locks us into the moment,

as does the bootylicious murmur of a woman's taut flesh
rubbing bodaciously up against silk, evokes sin-
ful dreams in men & women eye know—a politically incorrect
thought eye know, though true in the track of reality flow—
is seductive as kisses tonguing inside passion sweetly,
sucking sounds flowering inside locked mouths
as she pulls you deep into the volcano of her song,
bodies moving instinctively now, poetically, mysteriously,
bodies come alive in the moment—on time, not behind time—

as when poetry is poured into language, great sounds of music
scaffolding up buildings, architraves of syllables
hanging off edges of pursed lips, like dripping notes there,
can be heard building into an improvised cadenza as it flourishes

when sound is thrust into the sky as an inventive idea,
is like a wondrous sleek building—an eagle soaring above it—

architecture can create memorable language up there
pointing fingers up toward where religion swears God is,

where we know the spirit of great poetry sings & lives

GLOSSARY

Ajoupa . . . . In Martinique and Guadeloupe, a thatched open-air struc-
ture, typically made from banana leaves. Called "joupa" in
Creole.

Alizé . . . . French name for the Antilles trade winds.

Bonda Butt . . . . A woman's behind; a style of dancing in the French Antilles.

Bootylicious . . . . An African-American term meaning voluptuous, curvy, or
attractive, generally in reference to women's behinds.

Buba . . . . A loose shirt with long, wide sleeves worn by men and
women in West Africa.

Bwa-kabritt . . . . A large, hairy cricket living mostly in Martinique but also in
the countryside of Guadeloupe. Legend says they can predict
rain when they screech, and I haven't found this to be
wrong.

Caca . . . . African and West Indian slang for excrement, shit.

Colibris . . . . Hummingbirds. The variety found in Guadeloupe tends to
be black, green, and blue.

Diglossic . . . . Having two closely-related versions of a language, usually
one for formal occasions and one for everyday use.

Dolores . . . . A town in the Mexican state of Michoachan, Mexico.

Dolos . . . . A made-up word meaning to have a fun-filled, joyous time
while making love; to have a great orgasm.

Doodoo . . . . In Guadeloupe, a term of endearment for close friends or
lovers, as in "I love you, doodoo." In America, slang for
excrement, shit.

Feijoada . . . . The Brazilian national dish. A stew of black beans and a vari-
ety of meats, usually garnished with oranges and served with
rice and leafy greens.

Erzulie . . . . The Haitian Voodoo goddess of the sea and love.

Filo-plumes . . . . A made-up word that here means a seam of feathered words or a stream of musical notes.

Flue . . . . A pipe or tube through which air, gas, steam, or smoke can pass, as in a chimney.

Foo-foo . . . . A traditional West African food made by boiling and pounding starchy foods such as cassava, yams, or plantains. The finished product is then used to scoop up soups, stews, or sauces.

Gingembre . . . . A syrup mixture of ginger roots, sugar, water, and various fruits and plants. In Guadeloupe and Martinique, it is used as an ingredient in traditional rum drinks.

Gwo ka . . . . A family of traditional Guadeloupan hand drums; a musical style produced on gwo ka drums. Gwo ka music uses seven rhythms and is generally performed in a circle.

Hougan . . . . A Haitian Voodoo priest.

Karintha . . . . A character in *Cane,* by Jean Toomer. A beautiful woman, she is described as having skin "like dusk on the eastern horizon . . . when the sun goes down."

Lake Patzcuaro . . . . A lake in the Mexican state of Michoachan.

Lewoz . . . . One of the seven rhythms of gwo ka music; a performance, usually impromptu, of traditional gwo ka music in Guadeloupe and Martinique.

Loas . . . . Spirits typically used in the practice of Voodoo.

Al Loving . . . . An African-American abstract painter (1935–2005).

Mack-by-mack . . . . "Mack" is an African-American slang term meaning to flirt, or to speak persuasively. Here, mack-by-mack means "talk by talk."

Mofwazé . . . . In Guadeloupan legend, a human that has the ability to transform into a talking dog.

Moto-cell ....A made-up word playing on Motorola's "Moto" marketing campaign; a cell phone.

Moto-flow ....A made-up word playing on Motorola's "Moto" marketing campaign; flowing or moving in a technologically advanced manner, especially in reference to young people.

Pigology..............The culture of barbecue and pig lovers.

Pippiree ....A made-up name for an unknown West Indies bird, playing on the sound of its unique call.

Rapolic...............A made-up word describing anything pertaining to rap culture; an object, person, or situation that has characteristics of rap culture.

Rapology.............A made-up name for the ethos and philosophy of those involved in hip-hop and rap culture.

Soukougnan..........In West Indian folklore, a creature capable of shedding its skin at night, flying batlike, and emitting light.

ti punch..............In the West Indies, a small traditional rum drink ("ti" is short for *petit*, French for "small"). There are many variations, but the drink usually includes rum, sugar syrup, and lime.

Tout de suite..........French, meaning at once, immediately, right away.

Ylang-Ylang ....The flower of the cananga tree, native to Asia and imported to the West Indies; commonly used in perfumes and aromatherapy.

COLOPHON

The Architecture of Language was designed at Coffee House Press,
in the historic warehouse district of downtown Minneapolis.
The text is set in Kinesis.

FUNDER ACKNOWLEDGMENTS

Coffee House Press is an independent nonprofit literary publisher. Our books are made possible through the generous support of grants and gifts from many foundations, corporate giving programs, individuals, and through state and federal support. Coffee House Press receives general operating support from the Minnesota State Arts Board, through an appropriation by the Minnesota State Legislature and from the National Endowment for the Arts, a federal agency. Coffee House receives major funding from the McKnight Foundation, and from Target. Coffee House also receives significant support from: an anonymous donor; the Elmer and Eleanor Andersen Foundation; the Buuck Family Foundation; the Bush Foundation; the Patrick and Aimee Butler Family Foundation; the Foundation for Contemporary Arts; Gary Fink; Stephen and Isabel Keating; Seymour Kornblum and Gerri Lauter; the Lenfesty Family Foundation; Rebecca Rand; the law firm of Schwegman, Lundberg, Woessner & Kluth, P.A.; Charles Steffey and Suzannah Martin; the James R. Thorpe Foundation; the Archie D. and Bertha H. Walker Foundation; Thompson West; the Woessner Freeman Family Foundation; the Wood-Hill Foundation; and many other generous individual donors.

 This activity is made possible in part by a grant from the Minnesota State Arts Board, through an appropriation by the Minnesota State Legislature and a grant from the National Endowment for the Arts.

To you and our many readers across the country, we send our thanks for your continuing support.

Good books are brewing at coffeehousepress.org